The Little
Book of
Dreams

*For Anoushka F, my namesake,
who taught me to sleep,
perchance to dream*

The Little
Book of
Dreams

Anoushka F Churchill

An Hachette UK Company
www.hachette.co.uk

First published in Great Britain in 2020 by Gaia Books,
an imprint of Octopus Publishing Group Ltd
Carmelite House
50 Victoria Embankment
London EC4Y 0DZ
www.octopusbooks.co.uk

Distributed in the US by Hachette Book Group,
1290 Avenue of the Americas, 4th and 5th Floors, New York, NY 10104

Distributed in Canada by Canadian Manda Group
664 Annette Street, Toronto, Ontario, Canada M6S 2C8

ISBN 978-1-85675-422-4

A CIP catalogue record for this book is available from the British Library.

Printed and bound in China.

10 8 6 4 2 1 3 5 7 9

Publishing Director Stephanie Jackson
Art Director Juliette Norsworthy
Senior Editor Alex Stetter
Copy Editor Clare Churly
Design and illustrations Abi Read
Senior Production Controller Allison Gonsalves

Contents

1. Such Stuff as Dreams are Made on

What are Dreams?

There is, perhaps, no subject more studied than dreams. Humanity has been attempting to understand how and why we dream for thousands of years.

Of course, all the Abrahamic religions (mostly Judaism, Christianity and Islam) have dream stories in their holy books. But the *Epic of Gilgamesh*, a poem featuring the meaning of dreams, was written two thousand years before Christ came on the scene, and Aboriginal Australian folklore – known commonly as 'Dreamtime', or 'Dreaming' – is said to stretch back as far as sixty thousand years.

For as long as human beings have been able to record their thoughts, they have recorded their dreams and struggled to understand them: *why me?, why this dream?, what does it mean? and how can I use it?*

You have picked up this book because you, too, have wondered this.

Interpreting Dreams

Have you ever dreamed something horrible and then woken up, battered and baffled, wondering: what was *that*?, where did it come from? and what does it even mean? Perhaps you've dreamed about kissing Queen Elizabeth II and wondered if that meant you secretly had a weird fetish for royalty. Or maybe you've dreamed about being stuck in a lift with a man who was simultaneously your former maths teacher and your current boss, while knowing you needed to get to Caracas before five o'clock to deliver a parcel of bees, or your mother is going to kill you. (And was your teacher/boss flirting with you?)

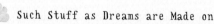

I'll level with you: I can't tell you what these dreams mean. Nobody can tell you for sure. We don't even really know what dreams *are*, or how they happen. We certainly don't know definitively what each individual dream might absolutely *mean*. Nobody does. The more we learn about the brain, the more we realize we just don't know.

So why read this book at all? Why bother? Well, because, over sixty thousand years, humanity has amassed a great many ideas about how dreams – so mysterious, yet somehow universal – can help us.

Over the course of this book, we'll find tools to interpret dreams for ourselves. These tools, drawn from everything from neurological hard science to spiritual beliefs, pull together the wisdom of all who came before us to give us the best possible chance of using our dreams for good.

EXERCISE:
Word Association

This exercise is an incredibly useful warm-up for thinking about dreams critically, analytically and interpretatively. This is because dreams work a lot like word association.

Below you'll find a space for a word association activity. Around the word 'dreams' in the bubble, jot down anything that the word 'dreams' calls to mind: clouds, pillows, the American Dream, night terrors, nightmares or perfect fantasies, it can be anything you like. Don't worry if you can't explain it – and definitely don't overthink it.

DREAMS

Do you see how your ideas spin off from one another? Do you notice how words can mean more than one thing at once? Sigmund Freud called this phenomenon 'condensation'. It is the idea that things can have many layers of meaning and complications, some useful, some not.

Dreams are all things to all people; real/unreal, art/science, personal/universal, routine/wonder, ourselves/not ourselves, prophecy/reality. They can affect many areas of our life in a very real way, whatever they are and whatever you believe.

You see, if you were to compare the results of your exercise with someone else's, you'd probably find some similarities – as well as some serious differences. Acknowledging this is key to understanding the problem with most books about dream interpretation – but this book is a bit different.

The Language of Dreams

There are lots of books that promise to 'decode' your dreams, as if your dream language might be the same as the author's. Now, it's possible that you and I may have similar dream languages, given that there are obvious points of similarity between us. We're both interested in dreams, for a start, which might suggest we share a sensitivity. Perhaps we're both people who think it's worth considering how we interact with the world. Let's go further: we both worry that we are running out of time to do everything we want, and we both feel that there's more to us than others necessarily see. Seem about right?

The great neurologist Matthew Walker, in his book *Why We Sleep*, describes an exercise he does with each new class he teaches, where he asks a random student to tell him a dream. The student is always amazed at the accuracy of Walker's interpretation. How does he do it? The solution is simple: he gives the same interpretation every time, whatever the dream. As with lots of fortune-telling tricks, the answer lies in the fact that the feelings he describes are common to almost everyone.

Dream interpretation that relies on basic human commonalities, without digging down further into the individual psyche, is pretty silly – and unlikely to tell us anything useful. But don't throw this book away just yet. We are, after all, such stuff as dreams are made on, and an understanding of our dreams can help us understand our own 'stuff' better. It can help us to know ourselves and our deepest desires and fears.

So how is this book different to those other books about dreams? Well, instead of providing a 'dictionary' decoding the meanings of individual dream symbols, it will talk us through various approaches to understanding different dream qualities.

Dream Qualities

In this book I've chosen to focus on several dream qualities, with tips, exercises and space for you to try things out for yourself.

We're going to start with how you *feel* in your dreams: your emotions, the simplest dream quality to interpret. Then we're going to look at what you're *doing* in your dreams: the plot, the story and the journey. After that, we'll focus on the people in your dreams, which can be the hardest quality to interpret. And once we've mastered interpreting those three qualities, we'll move on to using those dreams in our real life – including prophecy, projection and lucid dreaming.

But before we begin to examine those qualities, there are two things we need to consider: are we sleeping well enough to even *have* dreams?, and do we remember them when we wake?

In the next chapter we'll look at how to sleep better.

2. Rounded with a Sleep

Better Sleep, Better Dreams

We can't talk about dreams without talking about sleep. Specifically, we can't talk about dreaming better, or more usefully, without talking about sleeping better. Without good sleep it is impossible to have good dreams. Without good sleep, actually, it's impossible to do almost anything.

You probably know for yourself that it's harder to concentrate after a disturbed night; and that a number of disturbed nights in a row can make executive functioning almost impossible. Sleep, you see, is as vital as food or water; exhaustion as pressing a concern as hunger or thirst.

We understand what food and water give to our bodies: it's a simple in-out equation. Sleep is far more nebulous. We know that sleep triggers the release of a growth hormone that mends our muscles and tissues and promotes growth. We know that sleep allows proteins in our body to synthesize better, which promotes healing and improved function. We know that sleep allows adenosine – a by-product of brain cells' activities – to clear from our mind, and that this might be part of what restores us to peak mental fitness the next day.

Scholars, after studying the problem for many years, eventually concluded that sleep was defined by four things: a period of **reduced activity** and **decreased responses to stimuli**, taken in a **typical posture** (lying down, eyes closed), that was **easily reversible**. (That last one, presumably, is there to distinguish sleep from...well, death.)

If you're thinking that you could have written that description yourself: well, yes. You're probably right. The study of sleep is hampered by the researchers' inability to see into the minds of their subjects. Once again, the best person to observe your sleep is, in many ways, yourself.

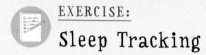

Sleep Tracking

Let's begin with a sleep-tracking exercise. We're going to draw up a simple chart, and use it to track just a few factors over a couple of weeks. And here's a stretch goal, if you feel like it: we're going to plot these values on the graph below.

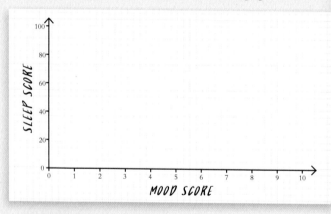

Tracking Your Sleep

Each day, we'll track the time we go to bed, the time we wake up and any periods of wakefulness (just jot down the time, if you wake up!). Then we'll work out how long we slept (excluding any wakeful hours) and rate the total sleep quality out of ten. To get your sleep score, multiply the hours slept by sleep quality. For example, if you slept for seven hours, with a sleep quality of six, you'd multiply 7 × 6 for a sleep score of 42.

Tracking Your Mood

At the end of the day, we'll rate our mood during the day out of ten. Things might have been tough for external reasons, but how did we handle it? Did we feel composed? Did we feel overly stressed? Did we cry on the way to work or feel like hiding underneath the bed? (A score of ten being flawless composure; one being hiding underneath the bed.) To get your mood score, simply take that reading out of ten.

Plotting the Scores

Plot the sleep score against the mood score, and make a little x on the graph. Do this for every day you track your sleep. You'll probably start to see a pattern emerge after a few days, but keep going for at least a couple of weeks: there is a clear correlation between quality of sleep and quality of life.

Improving the Quality of Your Sleep

Maybe the sleep-tracking exercise revealed a low score in sleep quality, and a low score in resulting competency, and you're wondering how to change this. Is this just your life? Is there anything you can do?

Of course there is.

First, you need a routine. To start signalling to your brain that it's time to wind down, get into the habit of taking a bath (a muslin bag filled with lavender and oats, tied with kitchen string, and dropped in the bath will release a soothing scent), dressing in pyjamas; and reading a real book (just like this one!).

No TV. No screens. And, if you can manage it, no phones in the bedroom at all. Blue light disturbs sleep because it tricks our brains into thinking it's the middle of the day, releasing chemical signals to promote wakefulness – the opposite of what we're after.

Ideally, you'd *never* have your phone in your bedroom, and certainly never in your bed. Remember the word association exercise (see page 10)? You don't want your brain to associate 'bed' with 'work', or even 'going out' – and you certainly don't want those blue lights! Make your bedroom a safe, clean, softly lit space that's dedicated only to sleep.

Sleep Problems

If you wake up during the night,
leave the bedroom. Go and read on the
sofa, or elsewhere – keep your bedroom for sleeping.
Similarly, never wear your day clothes on your bed.

If you often have trouble sleeping, it's worth mentioning
that alcohol doesn't help at all (passing out doesn't count as
sleeping, for neurological purposes) and coffee is a nightmare
as well (pardon the pun). Caffeine wakes you up by
temporarily blocking the flow of adenosine to the adenosine
receptors. The key word here, of course, is 'temporarily'.
When the caffeine dissipates, the brain has to process all the
built-up adenosine in a rush, instead of gradually, and thus
we get the so-called caffeine crash. This fact may, rightly,
make you somewhat wary of coffee.

And lastly, try not to worry about not sleeping too much.
I know. Much easier said than done. But think about babies,
who have no idea how to worry about sleeplessness and
sleep for something like 14 hours a day. Be like a baby.

Babies, in fact, may be the key to understanding why
sleep matters…

Sleep Stages

Sleep has four key stages: 1, 2, 3 and REM. The first two are light; the third is the deep, heavy sleep that has been said to restore the body; and the fourth is REM. We cycle through these stages in turn over the course of about 90 minutes, repeating for as long as we are asleep. So it seems obvious, then, that the more we sleep, the more REM sleep we'll get.

Unluckily, it's not as simple as that, because the cycles change through the night.

Our first sleep cycle is mainly comprised of deep sleep. This sleep stage is both the most necessary physically, and the hardest for us to wake up from, so our bodies do this part first as a kind of evolutionary priority. In the first 90-minute cycle, we get perhaps ten minutes of REM sleep. By the third sleep cycle, however, REM sleep takes priority – and after that we alternate mostly between light sleep and REM for the rest of the night.

The Importance of REM Sleep

The first four to six hours of our sleep, in some ways, is simply the time it takes for our brains to repair themselves – and it's only after that the body can begin its real dreamtime. If we skip that stage (by going to sleep too late or waking up too early), we don't dream properly.

So what does all this have to do with babies? Well, of the 14 hours that babies sleep per day, more than half is spent in REM sleep. For adults, this proportion is often less than a quarter. We learn more in infancy than at any other time, and it seems likely that this extended dream-sleep is at least part of the reason why.

We used to think our brain were inactive while we slept, but new research shows this isn't true. In fact, our brains are extremely active when we sleep. In what might be the world's cutest scientific study, researchers at the University of Chicago in 2009 demonstrated that 'baby birds practise new songs while they sleep'. Researchers were able to implant tiny electrodes into the brains of zebra finch chicks. By looking at the results of these electrodes, scientists were able to see neurological patterns in the way birds learn. Baby birds, it turns out, learn first by hearing themselves copy their parents – and then by dreaming about it.

The baby birds who were allowed to dream learned the songs; the birds who weren't allowed to sleep did not. Furthermore, the neurological patterns of their dreams corresponded exactly to the neurological patterns that occurred when they first heard the parent birds sing.
We think something of the kind happens in humans too: dreaming allows us to process the events of the day, and learn from it.

If dreams are what allow us to process and learn, then it's even more important that we should analyse them properly. In the next chapter, we'll learn how to make that happen.

3. Catching a Cloud

Remembering Dreams

How often do you remember your dreams? Everyone knows that dreams are hard to recall in precise detail. Like attempting to catch a cloud or holding water in your cupped hands, dreams that once seemed so tangible can slip away without your even noticing.

There are some people, in fact, who never remember dreaming. Maybe you're one of them, and you've come to this book to try and understand why. Don't worry. We'll look at the reasons we don't remember dreams, and learn some techniques to improve our recall.

Robert Stickgold, of the Harvard Medical School, has studied this problem extensively. People who don't remember their dreams tend to have similar sleep patterns to one another: sleep easy, sleep quickly, sleep deep and wake quickly to an immediate state of up-and-at-'em.

Researchers at the Lyon Neuroscience Research Center in 2013 recorded the electrical activity in the brains of a group of people, half of whom were 'high recallers' (who mostly remembered their dreams) and half 'low recallers' (who rarely did so). They found that high recallers tend to wake up for about 30 minutes per night; whereas low recallers were awake for just under half that time.

Stickgold's solution to this finding is somewhat unorthodox: he suggests drinking three large glasses of water before bed, to wake you up at frequent intervals during the second half of the night. This seems like a dedication to remembering your dreams that is at best likely to lend itself to a grouchy morning, and at worst rather risky. So what else can we do?

Well, the Lyon researchers found that high recallers were also more likely to respond easily, in their waking lives, to their name being called. In some sense, then, we can say that these people were more highly attuned to the waking world. Thus, improving our recall of the waking world can improve our recall of dreams.

Some dream theorists suggest that practising remembering real places can act as a kind of training ground for remembering dream places. Look out of the window for 60 seconds, concentrating hard on as many aspects of the scene as you can, then look away and try to recall every detail. Come back to this memory throughout the day, perhaps taking notes to compare your recollections after a minute, after an hour and after several hours. In this way, you can begin to train your brain.

You might notice, as you do this exercise, that memory can be helped and hindered. For instance, if you see something that reminds you of the scene you memorized, the memory will probably come back to you without much conscious effort. This is called the 'trigger effect', and it can be made useful to you in two ways: strengthening your brain's ability to recall things and allowing you to use a 'dream anchor'.

Strengthening Recall

To improve your recall, observe when something in your waking life triggers a memory, whether that's of your real life or a dream. Take care to notice these feelings, whether they manifest as a memory or as something like déjà vu, and note them down. You could even start making a kind of 'dream dictionary' of the feelings and ideas associated with places, objects or people. To do this, take a new notebook, and label each page alphabetically A–Z. As you start to notice the world around you, and the feelings triggered by that world, jot them down, adding to your notebook any time you have a fresh association or idea. We'll look at this idea more closely later in the book (see pages 42–7).

Creating a Dream Anchor

A dream anchor is an object that you focus on immediately when you wake, and as you meditate on the object you make a specific effort to recall the dream from which you have just awakened. It should be the first thing you focus on in the morning, and as you stare through and past the anchor you'll try your best to recall any dreams. This works by association: the more you do this, the more you'll associate the object with the successful recollection of dreams.

Some dream scholars suggest that a dream anchor can be as simple as a bedside lamp, candle or other object you have lying around – but creating one can be a fun and satisfying project that also allows you to focus your mind on your intentions. Focussing your intentions can be extremely powerful, particularly when we're dealing with questions of the subconscious mind.

Take some time to find or make a dream anchor that feels right to you. Mine, for instance, is a small bronze cube I found in a shop. You could embroider, paint, carve, draw or buy some small totem that feels right to you. As you're making it, or searching for it, focus your mind on the purpose and intention of the dream anchor: *this will help me recall my dreams, this will help me remember my dreams*. While repeating a mantra may seem like magic, it's based in the sound psychological principles of association, subconscious suggestion and determination.

After all, Robert Stickgold also suggests using a mantra before bed: *I will remember my dreams*. Repeat it out loud, while focussing on your dream anchor, as the last thing you do before you go to sleep. Try to believe it.

Dream Recall

The most useful thing you can do to improve your dream recall is to force yourself to sit and recall your dreams. You have to make dream recall a priority.

The moment you wake up, don't move, don't speak, don't turn to the person next to you and announce 'I had such a weird dream!' Instead, linger in the dream world as long as you can, with your eyes closed. Think, 'Where was I just now? What about before that? And before that?' Cling on to keywords for parts of the dream: *fire, flying, teeth, poodle, mother.* Then open your eyes, focus on your dream anchor while you try to recall every sensation, and – here's the key – immediately write the keywords in a dream journal you keep for the purpose.

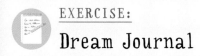

EXERCISE:
Dream Journal

A dream journal is the single most efficient way to improve dream recall; and therefore the single most useful tool we have in dream analysis.

We're going to break dreams down into five categories: the **cast of characters** (who was in the dream with you); the **set** (where the dream took place); the **props** (the objects in the dream); the **action of the dream** (what happened); and the **emotions of the dream** (how you felt about it).

Take a notebook and pen, and copy the template on the next page.

To begin with, we'll consider the prompt questions. We'll scribble down keywords to jog our memory, then go back and fill in the gaps. Once we're done, we'll give the dream a title that reflects what we've written. The title will help us cement the dream in our memories, and provide an easy way for us to see if there are any recurring themes or patterns in our journal.

For now, we're going to leave the 'Awake' box empty. You'll learn how to use it later in the book (see page 44).

AWAKE:

DATE: ....

TITLE: ....

KEYWORDS: ....

....

....

CAST: ....

....

....

Who was there? Do you know them in real life? Do you know them well? What's their relationship to you, and was it the same in your dream? Did they look the same?

SET: ....

....

....

Where were you? Were you somewhere familiar or strange? What time of day was it? What time of year? Have you been to this place recently, a long time ago or never? Was it old? Was it new? What temperature were you?

PROPS: ....
....
....
....
....

What was there with you? What were you holding? What were you wearing? What material things made up this immaterial world?

ACTION: ....
....
....
....
....

What were you doing? Where were you going? What were you trying to do, or failing to do, or what did you say? Were you talking? Did you say anything that you can remember?

EMOTIONS: ....
....
....

How do you feel right now? How did you feel while dreaming? Is there a difference? Were these feelings linked to someone you saw in the dream, or where you were in the dream, or what you were doing in the dream?

4. Overnight Therapy

Emotions

Emotions are the simplest dream quality to interpret, even though they can be complex. Much expensive, sophisticated psychotherapy essentially boils down to a process of understanding what we are feeling at any given moment and in any given situation.

It can be so hard to identify exactly what we're feeling, in fact, that therapists often use a feelings chart, like the one on the following page, to help us pin it down.

FEELINGS CHART

Admiring	Disgusted	Indifferent	Regretful
Affectionate	Doubtful	Indignant	Relaxed
Alarmed	Eager	Insecure	Reluctant
Alienated	Embarrassed	Interested	Resentful
Angry	Enthusiastic	Jealous	Romantic
Annoyed	Envious	Joyful	Sad
Anticipatory	Excited	Listless	Satisfied
Apprehensive	Frightened	Loved	Shocked
Ashamed	Frustrated	Loving	Shy
Bitter	Furious	Lustful	Spiteful
Blissed-out	Glad	Melancholic	Stressed
Bored	Gleeful	Miserable	Sulky
Brave	Glum	Nervous	Surprised
Calm	Grateful	Nostalgic	Suspicious
Cheerful	Grieving	Outraged	Tense
Confident	Guilty	Overwhelmed	Terrified
Contemptful	Happy	Panicky	Thrilled
Curious	Helpless	Paranoid	Triumphant
Defeated	Hungry	Pitying	Wondering
Desiring	Hurt	Pleased	Worried
Detached	Hysterical	Proud	Yearning
Discontented	Impatient	Raging	Zealous

Humans have words for many gradations of feelings – and, furthermore, we can recognize them in others. We are finely calibrated to interpret facial expressions by mood.

The neurologist Matthew Walker, in his book *Why We Sleep*, explains how he showed a group of people many pictures of a face. The first picture of the face was friendly and open; the last picture was stern and threatening; and between them the pictures gradually shaded from the first face to the last, with minute differences in facial expression to convey emotion. The participants in the study were able (after a full night's sleep) to accurately assess the feelings conveyed in each image. When the experiment was repeated, and the participants were deprived of that sleep, they became unable to grade the photographs properly: they were unable to read the delicate nuances of each face.

Sleep and emotions are tied together in ways that perhaps we don't fully understand, yet understanding the emotions of our dreams can help us understand our waking lives. Dreams have even been called 'overnight therapy'.

Dreams and Emotions

We all know that there's a link between what happens when we sleep, and the way we feel. We know that a bad night's sleep makes us grouchy and irrational the next day. Many people even report carrying the emotions of their dreams into their waking lives. Our dreams and sleep, then, influence our waking emotions in many ways – but, of course, the converse is also true.

Emotions are the most thinly disguised of all the dream elements: if we feel shame in a dream, it's likely to be related to shame we feel in real life. There is a strong correlation between how we feel when we're awake and how we feel in our dreams.

This isn't to say that we'll necessarily feel the same about what we *do* in dreams as we might if we did them while we were awake – but we carry our emotions into our dreams with us. This is where almost all psychoanalytic dream assessment begins (think Sigmund Freud or Carl Jung), and it's backed up by science: studies have shown that when we note down the strongest emotion felt in our day, and the strongest emotion of our dreams, they are likely to be similar. Mark Blagrove, who led a team of researchers at Swansea University, found that events with high emotional impact were significantly more likely to be rehashed in dreams than events that meant less to us.

Let's demonstrate this for ourselves by carrying out a version of these experiments.

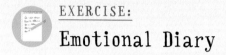

EXERCISE:
Emotional Diary

For this exercise, we need three things: a pen, our dream journal and the list of feelings from the chart on page 40.

Start by focussing on the 'Emotions' category in your dream journal, and that blank 'Awake' box at the top of the page (see page 36). Before you fall asleep, as part of your bedtime routine, consider the following questions, and write down your answers in the blank box, using the feelings chart to help you:

• *What was the strongest emotion I felt today?*

• *What triggered it?*

When you wake up in the morning, record your dreams in your journal and consider these questions:

• *What was the strongest emotional impression left by my dream?*

• *What triggered it?*

After a couple of weeks of this exercise, you'll probably start to see a pattern. Studies show that people suffering from stress are more likely to experience nightmares; and that people who report bad dreams are most likely to also report low levels of satisfaction with their waking life. This phenomenon is well documented scientifically – and is blindingly obvious to anyone who has ever had a nightmare. Our subconscious mind deals with the same stress levels as our conscious mind, so why shouldn't the same emotional preoccupations recur?

Happy People, Happy Dreams

Presumably exhausted by the field's obsession with the unhappy, three Australian scholars (Susan Gilchrist, John Davidson and Jane Shakespeare-Finch) attempted in 2007 to find a correlation between positive emotions and positive dreams. Happily, they succeeded: over half the participants recorded having pleasant dreams when they had had a pleasant day.

Moreover, the Australian researchers also found that there were 'significant correlations between some personality characteristics and participants' tendency to experience positive or negative emotions in dreams'. Broadly speaking, happy people have happy dreams; sad people have sad dreams.

To put it more finely, and more psychologically, if you're having repeated unhappy dreams, perhaps there's a difficult emotion in your waking life you're not processing properly. Freud believed that dreams were manifestations of repressed desires, often sexual desires, that go all the way back to childhood – but it doesn't have to be that complex. Is there something you want, but don't have?

This could be something tangible, but it could also be something like recognition or affection. Maybe you want to be acknowledged for your work, or for who you are. Maybe deep down you're lonely, stressed or unhappy in some other way.

Take a moment to look at your emotional diary (see page 44) and your dream journal (see page 35) and check in with yourself. Are there things you're not giving yourself the time or space to acknowledge? How could you best make that time? Where could you best find that space?

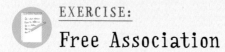

EXERCISE:
Free Association

An interesting way of checking in with ourselves and our deeper feelings is to play a word association game. You will need a pen and a piece of paper. Both Jung and Freud believed that this kind of work could bring out the deeper meanings behind dreams. Freud's technique is called 'free association'. Here's how we can use it:

First, decide on the strongest image you've taken from your dream. Maybe it's an object. Maybe it's a person. Maybe it's a place. This is your key symbol for the exercise. Write it down in the top-left corner of the sheet of paper.

What do you associate with that word? Don't think too much about it; don't worry if it doesn't make much sense. Jot your answers down in a kind of curve around the first word, like this:

What do you associate with all the new words? Write down those words too, like this:

Keep going, until eventually the page is full of words and pathways.

Do any of these pathways have a bearing on a real-life situation? Do any of these pathways speak to a particular need, want or desire in your life? Do any of the final words strike a chord with you in ways that weren't so clear in the original dream? Does this give you any ideas of where to go in your waking life?

This technique lets your mind wander freely, *prompted* by the original dream but without sticking closely to the specifics. (Jung's technique is much more interested in the dream itself, which we'll look at in the next chapter.)

Processing Strong Emotions

While free association might sound a bit wishy-washy, it is actually legitimate hard science. Specifically, it's been posited that it's all about a chemical called noradrenaline – the neuro equivalent of adrenaline. Adrenaline in the body is linked to fear and excitement and, essentially, a kind of overdrive. Noradrenaline does the same thing for the brain. Studies have shown that REM sleep is the *only* time that the brain is not actively producing noradrenaline.

People suffering from post-traumatic stress disorder (PTSD) have too much noradrenaline in the brain, and they often have repeated nightmares. However, when they take a drug to reduce the noradrenaline, the nightmares decrease radically.

It's important to note that nightmares can be useful. Matthew Walker considers researcher Rosalind Cartwright 'as important as Freud' on the understanding of dreams. Cartwright, Walker explains, carried out a series of psychological studies into the dreams of depressed patients going through a traumatic divorce. Those patients who actively dreamed about the traumatic feelings at the time were significantly more likely to be in remission from their depression a year later. The dreams helped the patients to distinguish the memory of the event from the vivid emotions associated with what happened.

When we remember hard times from our past, we don't feel the same strong emotions we felt at the time: we remember feeling the feeling, as it were, but not the feeling itself. 'I was so sad that day,' we might say, 'It felt so lonely there.' We are capable of talking about the past without reliving it – *unless* we have a condition like PTSD, *unless* we have too much noradrenaline, *unless* we aren't getting a chance to sleep properly and process the problems at the time.

Therapies like EMDR (eye movement desensitization and reprocessing) are now being utilized to help people who suffer in this way: by having the patient recount the trauma, while the therapist induces eye movements similar to those seen in REM sleep, we mimic the processing and 'filing' effects of dreaming.

Dreams make our past into stories. Dreams, according to some researchers, are what make our past into our past.

5. Dream Journeys

Our Dream Inheritance

'The dream acts as a piece of fiction that can be explored by the dreamer,' explains a 2019 study into the benefits of talking about our dreams, and that's what we'll look at now.

Some dream analysts, like Carl Jung, believe that all dreams are based on a series of deep stories called 'archetypes', common to all people and all cultures. Archetypes, in Jungian theory, are ideas and images that derive from the 'collective unconscious': things that crop up time and again in religion, myths and – yes – our dreams.

Jung believed that these stories were part of what it means to be human: that we are each born with an innate understanding of figures like 'The Mother' or 'The Trickster' and significant events such as 'The Apocalypse' or 'The Flood'. Jung believed that our dreams could be best understood as a new manifestation of those ancient patterns.

If you believe Jung, we inherit stories in the same way we inherit our body shape or senses.

Storytelling

Telling stories is how we make sense of the world, and it's how we make sense of our dreams too. Our waking mind constructs a narrative around the lingering images when we wake, which means that the dream is a collaboration between our conscious and subconscious. Sudden plot jumps, in dreams, are often the linking places between one dream and the next; it's just that we weave them together into a coherent narrative once we're awake.

Did the dream really
happen exactly as we narrate it?
Maybe not – how would we know?

But what's 'really' in this context? What's 'happen'? And does it matter?

The fact that a dream, once told, is a collaboration between our waking and sleeping selves – all parts of our consciousness – makes it *more* useful, not less. How is our conscious mind framing things dredged up by our subconscious? Could there be another interpretation? What other stories could we have told about this journey, or this action, and why did our subconscious present us with this interpretation? What does this say about us?

Falling or Flying?

One of the most universal dreams is the falling dream.
No, wait: the flying dream. No, wait: the falling dream.

These two dreams are sometimes referred to as two sides
of the same coin, which makes them a perfect case study.
Both are often triggered initially by similar physiological
factors, specifically the drop in heart rate and blood pressure
as we fall asleep. Both involve rushing through the air, not
touching the ground. The action of the dreams is similar,
yet the emotions underlying the dreams are very different.
We mostly wake up from flying dreams feeling elated, and
from falling dreams afraid. Our brain's interpretation of the
same electrical impulses tells us a lot about how we're feeling,
which gives us the tools to do something about it.

out of control   fear

downhill   falling into bed

falling on our feet   FALLING   falling from grace

falling short   falling asleep

falling off the wagon   falling in love   falling out

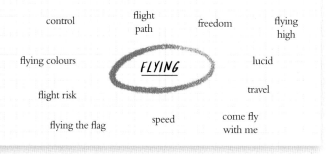

control

flight
path

freedom

flying
high

flying colours

FLYING

lucid

flight risk

travel

flying the flag

speed

come fly
with me

When we look at the words on the opposite page, we can see that falling isn't always negative. Sometimes letting go of control is a good thing – too much control can hinder us. Do we need to hold on? Can we let ourselves fall? What will happen if we do? It's said that you'll die if you hit the ground in a falling dream, which definitely isn't true, but sometimes when we fall, we fly…

Dream Actions

We've learned already how to sleep, recall our dreams and track our emotions from sleep into our waking lives and back again. Emotions are easy to translate (although, of course, not always easy to solve!) and that's why we started there.

Our actions can be harder to understand: the plots of our dreams (like the cast of characters, like the objects and places that surround our sleeping selves) are symbols. All dream analysts treat these symbols as a language we can decode individually, by asking ourselves why these actions, objects and people have surfaced for us now. What do they mean when taken in conjunction with our life now, our past and what we hope for in the future?

You'll notice that this book has lots of questions, and not many answers. That's because the most important part of dream analysis, like all therapy, is what *you* think and how *you* feel. No book can give you the answers: all this one can do is help you find them for yourself.

On the following page there is a questionnaire you can use to interrogate your dream actions – and learn more about yourself in the process.

EXERCISE:

Action Questionnaire

This exercise will help you answer the questions posed in the 'Action' category of your dream journal (see page 37) in greater depth, and in a more complex fashion. You might want to jot some of your answers down on paper first, to help you work out what's important.

Emotion

- *Do you view your behaviour in your dream with shame, or with compassion?*

- *Is your 'dream self' behaving in ways your waking self approves of?*

- *Do you wish you could behave like that, or do you feel regret?*

Who's in Charge?

- *Agency is the capacity to effect a change: to choose to do something and do it. Do you have agency in the dream?*

- *Does your 'dream self' want to be doing this?*

- *Are you doing it, or is it being done to you?*

- *Are you passive or active, subject or object, followed or following?*

Get Real!

- *Is this something that's possible in real life?*

- *Is the dream mimicking your recent real life, or is it further away?*

- *Have you ever done this activity?*

- *Do you want to do this activity? Why?*

- *Is this something you are afraid of?*

- *Would you be afraid of it in real life?*

- *Is this a fantasy?*

On the Move

- *What's the dream journey here?*

- *Where have you gone?*

- *Where have you come from? Why?*

- *What do both those places mean to you?*

- *Have you ever been there in real life?*

- *When did you go there in real life?*

- *Why were you travelling in the dream?*

- *How were you travelling in the dream?*

- *How did you feel about the journey?*

6. Cast and Crew

Who's Who in Dreams?

Gestalt theory is a kind of therapy that emphasizes a holistic approach to the self (that is to say, looking at the whole person). So it's no surprise that it's from Gestalt that we take this maxim: *we are everyone in our dreams.* Nobody else is in our minds; nobody else can dream for us. Each person in our dreams is our projection of that person: they are a composite of our ideas about that person, our ideas about their role in our lives and our ideas about their relationship to us. They are a representation of what we think of that person (or what that person represents), crafted by our subconscious from many sources.

Think of it like a puppet show, with your subconscious as writer, director, producer and star.

Cast and Crew

Sometimes the people-puppets in our dreams represent themselves – or, at least, our ideas of them. Often this is the case when we dream of people we recently saw, or had cause to think of in our waking lives: the dream is simply reproducing real life. They seem, in the dream, pretty realistic simulacra of our friends, colleagues, family, whoever. They don't act in ways that seem too surprising; and even after we wake we aren't too shocked by their dream presence or dream actions.

This seems fairly straightforward, and it can be – but beware! They are still just puppets, and they are still just us. They are still comprised of our ideas about what they are, who they are and who they are to us. We have to keep this in mind for two reasons. First, and most obviously, because people are more than our ideas about them. They can think and speak and feel for themselves – and believing our opinion of them to be the *only* opinion that counts is the fastest way to ruin a relationship. Second, by ignoring the things the characters in our dreams *represent*, we're ignoring important symbols: important messages from our subconscious.

The Five Elements of the Self

We've agreed that we are everyone in our dreams. Let's take this one step further: what if the characters in our dreams each represented different fragments of ourselves?

This kind of thinking is mostly drawn from Jungian dream analysis. Unlike Freud, Jung didn't believe dreams were about repressed sexual traumas: he believed that dreams were the key to understanding our subconscious wants, desires, stories and personal development. Jung wrote that there are five elements of self: anima, animus, shadow, persona and self.

Anima is the feminine; animus the masculine. Shadow is the darker parts of our personality: the enemy, the frightening parts of ourselves we don't want to acknowledge. Persona is our mask: who we are to the outside world. And the self? Self is who we truly are.

These five archetypes are sometimes said to be the ones who drive the people in our dreams: the puppeteers, if you like, behind those other characters. They might look like other people, they might look like strangers, but they are shaped and crafted by the elements of the self.

The difficulty, of course, is in knowing which is which. How do you know who each character represents?

How do you know what part of your subconscious is making itself known?

The answer lies, as usual, both in keeping a dream journal and in applying some Jungian analysis.

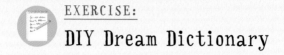

EXERCISE:
DIY Dream Dictionary

Remember those keywords we've been writing in our dream journal (see page 35)? We're going to analyse them now. You'll probably need a piece of paper, a pencil and a dictionary and thesaurus or access to the internet.

Take your first keyword. Write down anything immediately associated with it. For example, 'fire' might take you to 'hot', 'roaring', 'comforting', 'bright' or 'dangerous'. So far so good? This time we're not going to spiral out as we did with the free association (see page 48), but instead keep checking back in with the symbol. This is direct association.

Consider drawing the keyword: does that bring up any other associations for you?

Look up the word in a dictionary or a thesaurus, or search it online. Do you feel a resonance with any definitions, synonyms or common links?

Do the same for each keyword you wrote down, remembering all the time to bring it back to the keyword itself. What we're doing here is making a kind of dictionary of what each symbol means for you.

After a while you will start to see patterns: things that reoccur a lot for you. You might see patterns in a single dream, or you might see them over the course of time. This process is as unique as we are, and it allows us valuable insight into what our mind dwells on when freed from regular life.

Understanding Archetypes

Part of what we were looking for in the exercise on the previous page was those archetypes we touched on briefly before (see page 53). Often, they manifest as people – or as types of people.

If you've ever studied any kind of storytelling, you'll already be familiar with lots of these character types. They exist in fairy tales, myths and legends, and they feature heavily in religious stories. You might have come across them as part of spiritualism, say the Tarot deck, or you could have encountered them in the workplace: what is the Myers-Briggs Type Indicator questionnaire, after all, except a method for sorting people into characters?

Of course, people are more than one thing — especially in dreams. We're all familiar with the way in which someone can be two people at once in a dream — your mum and your doctor, or your sister and the window cleaner. This process is called 'condensation', and it means that our brain merges symbols together when dealing with a complex issue.

For example, your mum being one with your doctor might mean you're hoping that an upcoming hospital trip will take care of you (as a mother might). That's obvious, right? But it could mean that you're starting to look at your relationship with your mother the way a doctor might (clinical, detached); or that your relationship with your mother *is* sort of clinical, or detached, and that's worrying you. It might mean any number of things. This is why there's no point in most dream dictionaries. What you need is a way to explain how these archetypes relate to *you*.

It's worth noting that some of these archetypes might seem old-fashioned – but they're worth considering anyway. It's also worth saying that the so-called 'masculine' and 'feminine' energies are present in all of us. However, we live in a gendered society where different kinds of people are praised for prioritizing certain traits, which means, of course, that our dreams may be gendered too.

On the following pages are some archetypes drawn from a wide range of sources. Which ones have appeared in your dreams lately? Which ones are relevant to you? Who in your life can you match to these archetypes? Who would represent each one for you? Have a look at the list, consider and jot down any additional notes in your dream journal (see page 35).

The Fool

(aka The Innocent,
The Jester, The
Beggar, The
Child, The
Protagonist)

In traditional Tarot
archetypes, The
Fool often represents
you: a person about to
go on a journey. It may hint
at an optimistic desire for new
beginnings, or a need for new
beginnings. When this figure
shows up in your dreams, it
might be you, it might
be a child or it
might even be an
animal. Often
The Fool is
accompanied by
a little dog.

The Orphan

(aka The Martyr, The Child, The Outcast)

The Orphan is the central figure in so many stories, and has a lot to do with The Fool. Whereas The Fool tends to be a happy figure in dreams, The Orphan tends to be a bit of a pessimist: a loner, worried that they have been rejected, worried that nobody wants them. While everyone feels like this sometimes, to dream repeatedly of being orphaned suggests a fear of being outcast – and a fear of being alone.

The Warrior

(aka The Hero, The Protector, The Crusader, The Rescuer)

This archetype is often represented by somebody tough but kind; somebody capable of using great strength. If this kind of character shows up in your dreams, consider whether you are asking for protection or whether you want to protect someone else.

The Lover

The important thing to remember when dreaming of lovers is that love is love. Dreaming about sex doesn't always mean sex, just as death doesn't always mean death. Dreaming of lovers can hint at a need to compromise, a need to be more yielding, a need to be kinder. Dreaming of sex, for Jung, might indicate a conflict with that person that needs to be solved; or it might indicate a wish to become closer or more similar to a sexual partner. (An aside: everyone has weird sex dreams – try not to worry about it. It almost definitely doesn't mean what you think.)

Death

Just like sex doesn't always mean sex, death almost never means death. Sometimes, of course, we're rehashing the elements of our daily lives – we can dream about death after a bereavement, but that's not what we're looking at here. (See page 50 for more on the trauma-processing element of dreaming.) The figure of Death can appear in lots of guises – a traditional skeleton, a psychopomp (a mythical figure who escorts souls to the afterlife), a friend who has passed on – and often it indicates a need for change. Change is always a kind of death (and death the biggest change of all).

The Mother

(aka The Goddess, The Divine Feminine, The Caregiver)

Strongly connected to the anima part of our psyches, according to Jung (see page 66), The Mother tends to be related to caregiving more than actual motherhood. Dreaming of our mother might actually mean we're dreaming of needing to give or receive care; of a love without judgement. If we believe Jung, dreams about this figure aren't so much about our own mothers (who aren't all perfect goddesses!) as our instinctive understanding of the maternal.

The Father

(aka The King, The Priest, The Masculine)

The counterpart to The Mother, The Father represents the animus part of our Jungian psyche (see page 66). Often historically related to issues of control and authority, this figure might show up as a boss, a headteacher or other power figure. (Yes, this labelling isn't ideal – but so much of our subconscious is shaped by a flawed society.)

The Hermit

(aka The Scholar, The Student, The Hierophant, The Institution)

Often represented by priests, doctors, academics, schools, and hospitals, this archetype indicates your relationship with institutions and authority. It can also indicate a desire for spiritual or religious guidance; a desire to know where we're going; a desire to learn and to understand. It shows a desire to pull away from ordinary life into the life of the mind. Why might this be manifesting in your life? Are you overwhelmed by demands? Do you feel unrecognized for what you've done, and swamped by what you've still to do?

The Stranger

The Stranger might represent
parts of yourself you haven't yet
unlocked – or parts of yourself
you're uneasy about recognizing.
It's a common myth that we can't
invent faces: that everyone in our
dreams is drawn from someone
we once saw in real life, even if
we don't recognise them. In 2015
an internet hoax convinced
thousands of people that
thousands of others had seen
the same face in their dreams.
It claimed that thousands had
reported meeting the same man
in their dreams, as if the man
could travel into the minds of
many strangers. It was widely
reported, and many people
believed it before it was
debunked. But why did this
story appeal to so many of us?
Why did it ring so true?

Seeking 'Real' Meaning in Our Dreams

We want to believe that the dreams we have are signifiers of something tangible and real. For example, if we see a stranger in our dreams (see page 81), we want to believe it means something more than a random face generated by rogue electrical impulses. And who knows? That might be the case. In the next chapter, we'll look briefly at how that could be…

7. Shamans, Soothsayers and Lucid Dreamers

What is Lucid Dreaming?

Lucid dreams are those dreams where you know you're dreaming – and stay dreaming. Often the realization that you're dreaming can wake you (especially in nightmares, thank goodness), but it's possible to train your brain to stay awake and manipulate the dream into something great.

Once they know they're dreaming, lucid dreamers can take control of the dream. At its best, lucid dreaming is essentially like having superpowers. Everything you've ever wanted to do in real life, you can make happen in your dreams. Flying. Falling in love with a famous person. Seeing places you've always wanted to visit and doing things you've always

wanted to do. All of these are possible. It's like homegrown virtual reality, with none of the expensive equipment.

The Greek philosopher Aristotle wrote about self-awareness in dreams, which is at the heart of lucid dreaming. Knowing yourself, your brain and your dreams well enough to understand what's a dream and what's reality is immensely helpful for encouraging lucid dreaming (one reason it's so good to keep a dream journal, as we've been doing throughout this book). Knowing that you're dreaming gives your imagination the chance to manipulate and exert conscious control over a dream in an environment that feels almost fully real.

Lucid Dreaming as Therapy

Some researchers have suggested that lucid dreaming could be a valuable tool for therapy. Imagine being able to confront someone from your past who has hurt you in a safe and secure way; imagine the closure you could gain from that kind of experience. Imagine being able to probe your phobias in order to more deeply understand why you've been afraid – without ever having to, say, get on a real plane or touch a real spider. Lucid dreaming has even been used to help people suffering PTSD, although research is still in the early stages.

Studies with an MRI machine have started to be able to predict the dreams of certain volunteers, based solely on the ways their brains light up as they sleep, as Matthew Walker reported in *Why We Sleep*. While we can't yet apply this universally, imagine the possibilities! Imagine if we could induce certain dreams for certain people in a therapeutic sense.

We began this book by articulating just how much we don't know about dreams, and that's definitely true. But what that gives us is the possibility of an extraordinary future – one that can draw on the traditions of the past. Until then, however, we'll have to try to do it ourselves. On the next page, you'll find some tips for lucid dreaming, whether you want to use it for therapeutic reasons or just for fun...

Tips and Tricks for Lucid Dreaming

If you've followed the tips for better sleep and dream recall (see pages 20 and 31), you're already ahead of the game. Studies have shown that the better your dream recollection, the more likely you are to experience lucid dreams – so keep up with that dream journal.

Set Your Intention

It can be helpful to set an intention: a mantra of not just *I will remember my dreams*, but *I will notice when I am dreaming*.

Be Mindful

Mindfulness is the real key to lucid dreaming. In your waking life, ask yourself a question like 'Is this real?' or 'Is this a dream?' to build that question into the pattern of your day-to-day mind. That way, you'll dream the same question, and hopefully, over time, become aware of the differences between sleeping and waking.

Look at Your Hands

Another common trick is to look at your hands. It's hard for your brain, apparently, to accurately dream your own hands, so it can be a really significant 'tell'. If you build in looking at your hands to your daily life, you're likely to dream the same thing – and you're likely to notice a difference.

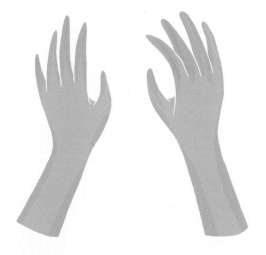

Focus on a Subject

If you want to dream about a particular subject, spend some
time thinking about that subject before bed: look at pictures,
read books, build up a full mental picture as if you've just
seen the person or place yourself.

Make Time for Dreaming

You're mostly likely (at least in my experience) to lucid
dream as you're falling asleep, or just as you're waking up,
so try to build some extra time for bed into your routine.
You know that swirly dark pattern you see just before you're
falling asleep? That's your hint to try and imagine something
you'd like to dream. It probably won't work straight away,
but keep at it.

Shared Dreaming

The next stage of lucid dreaming is often thought to be something called shared dreaming, or dream telepathy. Shared dreaming is, of course, being able to meet with other dreamers. Shamans, or dream walkers, profess to be able to go into the dreams of others. Some even claim to be able to influence those dreams. Is it possible? Many cultures believe so. Certain Australian Aboriginal tribes, for example, have deep and profound beliefs in the ways the spirit can leave the body and commune with others.

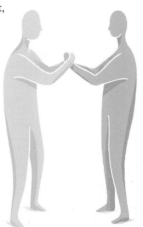

These stories and ideas are ancient, deeply felt and truly important, so it seems ludicrously arrogant that we should rule it out completely. After all, how could we confirm or deny the reports of what people dreamed? How could we be sure that they were truly experiencing the same dream and not just similar dreams based on similar environments? How can we, with the technology currently available to us, even begin to parse the vast complexities of the human brain? Many people report things from and about their dreams we just can't support with science, but that doesn't mean they're not true.

Often things that once seemed strange or primitive are now revealed to be scientifically sound. In the same way that chewing the bark of a willow tree was once thought to cure headaches, then reviled as a myth, then hailed as the wonder drug aspirin, might the same not be true of what we understand about dreams?

The Native American Iroquois, for instance, believe that dreams (particularly nightmares) must be banished by the whole tribe together, in a series of rituals, to stop harm coming upon them. People must come together to explore the elements of the dream to, in a sense, banish it. While this practice might once have been mocked, studies have now shown there is therapeutic benefit to discussing nightmares. There is a clear path from acting out the things that frighten us to absolute, scientific harm-reduction.

What else might we not know? What else might we have dismissed? How else might our dreams be useful to us in ways that currently we just can't prove?

Prophetic Dreams

Dream telepathy is, of course, linked to prophecy and prediction – and dreams have been part of prediction and prophecy for millennia. The *Epic of Gilgamesh*, written in the 7th century BCE, was prompted by a prophetic dream. The Ancient Egyptians wrote dream dictionaries (dreaming of warm beer, for instance, promised harm) and the Ancient Greeks created a complex dream-analysis system whereby dreams were classified as 'false' or 'true', with true dreams further subdivided into 'symbolic', 'vision' or 'oracle' dreams, as categories of prediction.

Many ancient holy books are full of dreams that change the course of history. But not just history: these dreams change the course of the lives of the individuals concerned. The dream changes the dreamer: it changes the dreamer's mind about what they should do, where they should go and who they should be. The dream has no power alone, but must be acted upon — on waking — by the dreamer.

Perhaps, then, this is one thing we can take away from the history of prophecy: dreams have the power to change our lives, if we let them. The lessons we learn from our dreams can shape us: the lessons we learn about ourselves, and the lessons we learn about the ways we view the world, and our place in it.

Just look at what we've learned about from this little book alone. How to sleep better. How to look properly at the world around us. How to keep a journal, and record things that are important to us. How to notice how we feel, and wonder why we feel it, and how to identify those feelings. How to understand ourselves (our wants, our desires, our needs). And once we know ourselves, we will know how to act. We will know how to change our lives to accommodate those needs and desires. We will know how to go through the world, secure in our understanding of people and place and self.

Self-knowledge is self-care, and self-care is radical: caring for the self allows us to be in the best possible place to care for the world around us. And what more could anyone want, from a dream, than that?

Acknowledgements

Thank you to Chad, the first therapist to teach me about sleep hygiene. Thank you to my doctor, Emma, for first introducing me to many of the ideas in this book. Thank you to the many analysts, therapists, experts and dreamers who I consulted in the process of writing. Thank you to the neuroscientists making such extraordinary strides in our understanding of the human mind. And a particular thank you to the scholars who make their writing accessible to the non-scientist!

Thank you to my editors for all their patience while I worked on this book, and for letting me write about something I am so passionate about.

Thank you to Hannah, Lottie and Libby for a lifelong commitment to talking about our dreams in depth. Thank you to my namesake, Anoushka F, the strangest dreamer of them all and queen of sleep. This book is in honour of your dedication to ten hours a night.

Above all, thank you to Therese, chief cheerleader of gentle days and herbal baths. I could not have written this without you.